Celtic Spells

Celtic Spells

How to walk the magical pathways of power

Marie Bruce

ARCTURUS

ARCTURUS

This edition published in 2022 by Arcturus Publishing Limited
26/27 Bickels Yard, 151–153 Bermondsey Street,
London SE1 3HA

Copyright © Arcturus Holdings Limited

ISBN: 978-1-3988-1077-8
AD008722UK

Printed in China

Contents

Introduction

Cead Mile Failte!

One hundred thousand welcomes!

*F*ailte, or welcome, to the mystical realms of Celtic magic. I will share with you the wisdom of the Celts, drawn from the four corners of Britain and the Celtic regions of Scotland, England, Ireland and Wales. Here you will learn more about the ancestry of the British Isles and the proud and powerful race of people known collectively as the Celts.

The Celts are renowned for being an often romantic, and sometimes brutal, community. In both history and mythology, they have given us many legendary kings and queens, warriors and heroes. From Robert the Bruce and William Wallace to Mary, Queen of Scots and Rob Roy Macgregor, to Cuchulain and Sgathaich/Scathach, many of Britain's warrior poets hail from the Celtic regions. Indeed, the term 'warrior poet' itself comes from Irish and Scottish folklore and refers to a chivalrous soldier who fights with mind, body and spirit, documenting his deeds in poetry. This lasting legacy remains evident in the literature of the war poets of the last century.

More than that, the Celts were also master magicians and artisans, leaving their sacred artwork dotted around the landscape for us to enjoy and wonder at. Pictish standing stones carved with intricate Celtic knotwork and imagery, such as the Eagle Stone in Strathpeffer, Scotland, still hum with ancient magic. There is a mystery and a magnetism about these stones, imbued by our forefathers, which we can still feel today.

Pictish standing stone.

As a Bruce, I have always been deeply drawn to my Scottish Celtic heritage and I have studied the legends, mythology and magic of Britain's Celtic regions for many years. Much of this book is a result of my time spent in Scotland, where the past is very much present and magic flows through the ancestral landscape. There is a tangible feeling of mysticism when crossing the border into any Celtic region, be it Scotland, Wales or Cornwall, which the intuitive naturally feel. To me, it feels like passing through a portal into a beautiful and enchanted realm. I want to share this feeling with you in the pages of this book.

For those of you who live in the UK, I want to show you how magical a staycation can be, while for those readers who live in other parts of the world, I want to tempt you to visit our sacred Celtic shores. But even if you can't travel to a Celtic country, you will be able to use the teachings of this book to bring the magic of the Clanlands into your own home through its spells, wherever you happen to live.

The Celts have much to offer. From them we can learn how to live like warrior poets in our own lives, how to maintain a calm courage in the heat of battle, and how to remain true to ourselves and steadfast in the face of betrayal and adversity.

In *Celtic Spells*, I will show you how to summon the blessings of the Four Winds, how to work spells with heraldic totems – the Red Dragon, the Red Lion Rampant and the Unicorn – how to invoke Celtic archetypes such as Scathach, the Cailleach and the Morrigan. You will learn how to use the symbolism of the Celtic Cross to come to a decision, how to create a Clootie tree in your garden, and much more. In this book I have endeavoured to excavate the strands of history, myth and magic drawn from the heart of Celtic culture and weave them together into a practical guide to modern spellcraft, with an ancient Celtic twist.

I hope that you enjoy this journey into the Clanlands of the Celts.
Blessings be upon you,
Marie Bruce x

Chapter One

CELTIC CULTURE

In ancient times, before the rise of the Roman Empire, the whole of the British Isles was ruled by a single people made up of many tribes. These people were the Celts. Their influence stretched beyond Britain, far into Gaul, which is modern-day France, Brittany in particular, parts of the Germanic regions, and Spain, where the Gaels were the predominant Celtic tribe. Great swathes of Europe were under their dominion and they were the dominant force prior to the Roman invasions.

Much of what we know about the Celts is based on conjecture, speculation, examination of ancient artefacts and educated guesswork. Historians and archaeologists have long been fascinated by the ancient Celts, though there is much debate surrounding the topic, including when they first came to settle in Britain. It is thought to have been around 600 BC, though some claim that it was much earlier.

However, one thing they all seem to agree on is that the Celts have left a rich heritage of history, art, music and language that we can explore, gaining an insight into our ancient ancestors. For make no mistake about it, there isn't a corner of Britain that wasn't shaped in some part by the Celts. Their sacred stones stand majestically across the land. Their artistic knotwork, skilfully carved into the rock by master craftsmen long ago, still glistens in the rain and frost. The sound of the pipes, once played in the march against Roman armies, continue to be played in modern conflict zones. Then, as now, whether they be Scots, Welsh or Irish instruments, when you hear the skirl of the pipes, you know that the Celts have arrived! But just who are the Celts, and what place do they have in modern magic?

ANCIENT MYSTICS

The Celts were a pagan culture and like many other shamanic people, they set great store by ceremony and ritual. They wore animal skins, feathers, claws and bones, not just for practical reasons, but also to connect with wild creatures as totems. Even today, you can see many a Scotsman wearing an eagle claw or hawk feathers on his brooch, to hold a ceremonial tartan in place. Vintage sporrans were often fashioned from the heads of animals such as foxes, badgers or wildcats. Totems were a part of the Celtic culture, invoking the spirit of animals to bring about greater cunning, ferocity or wisdom.

There is evidence to suggest that sacrifice was also an aspect of their culture too, and while the modern mind recoils from such a notion, in ancient times, sacrifice of both animals and humans was quite common, as it was thought to ensure the survival of the tribe by giving a life to the gods. These days, the sacrifice made in Celtic spells is symbolic, so you might give a gift of silver to the river to bring about prosperity, or leave an apple at a standing stone as an offering.

ANCIENT TRIBES

The Celts were a tribal race, often intermarrying and trading with neighbouring tribes – and warring with them too, until the arrival of the Romans gave them a common enemy to fight. From the Caledonii up in Scotland to the Brigantes in the north of England, to the Trinovantes and Iceni in East Anglia and the Dumnonii in Cornwall, to name just a few, Celtic tribes once lived throughout Britain. They were not just confined to the regions we think of as being Celtic today – Scotland, Ireland and Wales – although we can see echoes of the tribes in the more recent Clan system of those regions.

The arrival of the Romans threatened, and ultimately destroyed, this ancient tribal culture, and yet we still remember the names of those royal Celts who stood against the Roman invasion: Caratacus, Cartimandua and, most notably, Boudicca or Boadicea. These names echo across our own time, heroic by-words for standing against oppression, no matter what the consequences might be. This legacy is their Celtic battle-rage, forever stamped indelibly into our history like the blue woad tattoos Boadicea herself might have worn.

ANCESTRAL VOICES

Like many shamanic tribes, the Celts believed in the power of their ancestors and in a life after death. Archaeologists have unearthed evidence of death rituals, such as sacred last meals and unusually positioned bodies. Many grave goods have also been found, particularly

Ancient Celt houses called Castros in Galicia, Spain.

in bog-body burial sites around the UK, where they are preserved by the bog. These grave goods include jewellery, pottery and weaponry, indicating that the Celts believed their loved ones would have need of these items in the afterlife. It also indicates that they continued to feel a close connection with their loved ones after they died and wanted them to have all the comforts of home in eternity.

This focus on ancestral connections is not unusual in shamanic tribes. It is also prevalent in Native American, Mauri, Inuit and other indigenous tribes. It is an integral aspect of Celtic culture, in that *the past remains present*. By this I mean that the past is regarded as being a part of our own time and not separate from the present day. It is the warp and the weft of the fabric of life, on which our current day to day tapestry is being stitched. We are, each of us, a thread in the tapestry

Bog and heather in Scotland, where peat-bog bodies have been found that give us more information on the Celts.

of our Clan and in their story as it continues to unfold. This effectively means that you can never be without Clan, for you will always have your ancestors watching over you and guiding you on your path. You can strengthen this connection by creating an altar or sacred space dedicated to your ancestors.

BLOOD AND BONE ALTAR

Find a quiet space in your home to set up an altar to your ancestors. If you are part of a recognised Clan, lay a piece of Clan tartan over the surface as an altar cloth – so I would use the Bruce tartan. If you are not of a Clan, you can use any kind of altar cloth that pleases you. Black is a good choice because it represents the darkness of death and the unknown aspect of the afterlife. Next, light two white candles and place these towards the back of the altar. Now gather together anything that reminds you of your ancestors – for me, with Celtic heritage, this might be knot-work jewellery, a piece of antler, perhaps a dirk (a type of dagger) – for you, it might be gifts from deceased loved ones, memorial cards and anything else that you hold sacred to your lineage. Arrange these items around the altar. Then place a photo or picture of your ancestors in the middle, between the two candles. This could be a photo of your grandparents or parents, or it might simply be a figure from history that you feel a strong connection to such as Boudicca, Robert the Bruce or William Wallace, for example. Light a stick of your favourite incense in offering and say:

By blood and bone

By hearth and home

I welcome my ancestors to this hearth-stone

Love whole hearted

Though long departed

I welcome you in and call you home.

You can use this altar for your Celtic magic spells and also to commune with your ancestors for connection and guidance. Remember that you can never be Clan-less, for your ancestors are always there. You are a valuable thread in their tapestry. How you live your life helps to keep the Clan moving forward, at the same time honouring the past and those who have gone before.

Even if you are not from a Celtic family, you can still honour the Celts by focusing on the ancient Celtic tribes of your region. So, for example, if you are from Yorkshire, your altar could focus on the Brigantes, the Celtic tribe of Yorkshire, while those living in Cornwall might want to focus on the Dumnonii. If you live in Boston, in the United States, you might choose a tribe from Ireland that represents the Irish communities in that city. In this way, you are honouring the Celts of your own area.

MODERN GLOBAL CELTS

Historical events of the 18th and 19th centuries such as the Highland Clearances, the Irish Potato Famine and the Transportations, meant that the more recent Celts travelled far and wide, settling in America, Canada, Australia, New Zealand and so on. This effectively means that there are people all over the globe who can claim a Celtic heritage and so the magic and mysticism of the Celts is an international culture, with many countries, far beyond Scotland, even hosting their own Highland Games each year. So, regardless of where in the world you live, you can tap into the ancient magic of the Celts and claim a degree of kinship with them.

BAGPIPES: WEAPONS OF WAR

It is impossible to think of the Celts without also thinking of the pipes, which are an important aspect of Celtic culture. From the fearsome Carnyx used by the ancient Celtic tribes of pre-history, to the bagpipes that we most commonly associate with today's modern Celtic culture, the pipes have been used for centuries as a musical battle cry and a call to arms.

The piper holds a special place in Clan history. Pipers have always been both highly respected by their own people and greatly feared by their enemies, making them a prime target on the battlefield. If an enemy could take out the piper, they would remove the beating heart of the opposition and morale would plummet. This is due to the fact that the pipes are far more than a musical instrument – they are a tool of power and propaganda. The head of a carnyx looming out of the mists must have been a fearsome sight indeed, enough to make even the boldest of enemies think twice before engaging in battle!

Bagpipes have long been used as a communication device. They were the mobile phones of their time, with merry tunes and funeral dirges being played to relay good and bad news to neighbouring Clans across the glens. As an instrument, they are used to celebrate births, marriages and special events, to make a ceilidh go with a swing and to honour and commune with the Celtic landscape. Witnessing a lone piper *playing to the glen* is a sight and sound to behold, fit to melt even the hardest of hearts.

Moreover, the pipes were also used on the battlefield to instruct the soldiers, giving musical orders to denote when to push forward or fall back, what formations to take and so on. Keeping up the morale of the army was the vital role of the piper – he was the heart of the operation, just as important as the flag under which he played.

This tactical use of the pipes in warfare is the reason they were outlawed after the battle of Culloden in 1745. From then on, bagpipes were known as a weapon of war. They are still in use today

A man playing the bagpipes in a castle setting.

by the British military, with Pipes and Drums bands playing at Regimental events and military tattoos. What is more, they are still used as a battle cry and a warning, with various Scots regiments in recent years hoisting up their flag and playing the bagpipes as soon as they arrived at a combat zone. A weapon of war indeed.

Notable Warrior Pipers

John Macgregor, known as the Piper of the Alamo, was an expat who played to boost morale during a 13-day siege in the Texas War of Independence. Such was his effect on the troops that the general of the opposition sent a message asking him to stop playing. Of course, Macgregor refused, and played on.

Daniel Laidlaw was a piper from the First World War. His company was ordered to go Over The Top (OTT), but morale was low due to gas attacks being prevalent and the men were understandably reluctant. Piper Laidlaw went OTT alone and promptly marched up and down the trenches, playing his bagpipes, stirring up the hearts of the men, until they too went OTT and engaged with the enemy forces. For his bravery he was awarded the Victoria Cross.

William Millin, known simply as Piper Bill, was the piper who famously played to keep spirits up during the D-Day landings in the Second World War. He was immortalised with a statue in his honour at Sword, in France, to commemorate his courage and contribution to the war.

How to Use the Pipes in Ritual

While it takes years of study, practice and dedication to learn to play the bagpipes, you can still use them as a tool of power in your own life. Simply download or buy a CD of a selection of bagpipe music, and play it whenever you feel you need a morale boost to raise your spirits. Play the pipes whenever you have a personal battle to fight, be that a health scare, a messy breakup, a toxic work environment etc. Play the weapons of war and allow them to stir up your Celtic courage.

A Gallic soldier playing a carnyx.

Chapter Two

CELTIC MAGIC

C eltic magic is generally regarded as a type of traditional folk magic. It doesn't have the same high ceremonial aspect as Wicca, but it is very effective just the same. While you *can* cast a circle and call the quarters if you wish, as any Wiccan would do before performing spells and rituals, in Celtic magic this isn't considered necessary as the ancestors are deemed to protect us, rather than the circle. Celtic magic does have some similarities with Wicca and modern Paganism, most notably the festival sabbats and you can certainly incorporate some Celtic magic into your Wiccan practice if you want to. There is naturally some overlap, because modern Wicca has its foundation in old traditional folk magic, which the Celts would have been very familiar with.

CELTIC DRUIDS

It is impossible to separate the Celts and Druids, for they were all a part of the same ancient culture. The Druids played a key role in Celtic tribes. They were the recognised religious leaders and spiritual teachers. They were healers, using herbal remedies to tend to the sick and the dying. They were the law enforcers, managing disputes within and between the tribes and ensuring justice was served upon wrongdoers. The Druids were also warriors in their own right, frequently going into battle with their tribe. They were often regarded as Seers or Oracles, using divination to foretell the future of the tribe or warn of ill omens. They were well known for using a type of divination called

Augury, which is the art of studying the behaviour and patterns of birds to foresee events. Other animals could be used in a similar way. Boudicca, for example, preferred to use the movements of hares and rabbits to foretell if she would win or lose a battle.

The Druids were held in high esteem and were second only to tribal royalty and chiefs. They ensured that the gods were honoured, the festivals observed, and the history of the Celts was passed on to future generations. Unlike the Romans, however, they were not scribes and while the Romans documented everything, leaving a written legacy of their time, the Druids and Celts preserved their history through word of mouth, giving rise to one of their most iconic figures: the Bard.

Hares were used in a type of divination called Augury.

BARDS AND STORYTELLERS

The Celtic Bard is a rather romantic figure. We picture him waxing lyrical, holding his audience enthralled as they sit around a huge bonfire in the middle of a misty glen. This image might not be too far from the truth. The fact that this type of activity continued well into the Middle Ages and medieval period, giving rise to the traveling minstrels and troubadours who came after him, would indicate that the Bard was wielding a powerful tool of propaganda and entertainment. It was the Bard's responsibility to ensure that the history of the Clan was preserved in storytelling. He would weave together tales of victory in battle, interventions and signs from the gods, epic romance, encounters with the fey, enchanted weaponry and feats of magic.

Bards were also free to travel, to take the tales of their Clan further afield, to neighbouring Clans. In this way, they could act as emissaries and mediators.

They would gather news as they went, taking back vital intelligence to their chief, thus playing a key role in the politics, marriages, and battle plans of that time. Bards were warmly welcomed and enjoyed a certain amount of protection and privilege, much like the ambassadors of today. They had diplomatic immunity, meaning that they could not be harmed while in the territory of a rival Clan. All this political intrigue was carefully and diplomatically wrapped up in convivial entertainment. Each Clan or tribe would have their own Bard, and these men would have visited rival Clans, which must have made a pleasant change for the audience with an opportunity to hear fresh tales from a new voice, making the deep, dark cold of winter much more bearable.

This Bardic skill has never really disappeared, and modern Celts are still renowned for their ability to weave a good yarn. Think of Billy Connolly telling his tall tales on stage to make people laugh, or novelists such as Ian Rankin holding audiences enthralled with their words. The storyteller still plays a significant role in our society, from TV and radio script writers to authors, poets, musicians and so on. The power of the Bard is still prevalent in modern Celtic society too. Ask any Scotsman for directions and he will give you the history of every landmark you are likely to pass on the way to your destination! The Celts rarely get straight to the point because they will always have a long tale to tell. That is part of their charm.

Celtic Sabbats

The Celts observed the wheel of the year, honouring the turning of the seasons with a series of eight festivals, which are as follows:

Calen Gaeaf (31st Oct.) – this is the Celtic new year and the sabbat where we reflect on all that the past 12 months has brought. Ghost stories are a traditional part of this sabbat, as is carving out a turnip. In Cornwall it is also known as *Allantide*, a feast that honours the apple harvest and the cider that comes from it.

Alban Arthan (21st Dec., midwinter solstice) – traditionally this was the sabbat when the Druids would cut down mistletoe and bless it. We still honour this tradition today by hanging mistletoe in the home in December.

Gwyl Forwyn (2nd Feb.) – this is the feast of the maiden, usually represented in Celtic culture by the goddess Bride or Bridget. It is a time to welcome back the strengthening light.

Alban Eilir (21st March, spring equinox) – this is the time of the quickening, when the earth begins to show the first signs of spring. At this time, it was traditional to bless the seeds that were to be planted, be this a garden, a crop or a new goal or ambition. Bless the seeds for growth.

Calen Mai (30th April) – this sabbat is the feast of the May blessing, a time of union, fertility and coming together to enjoy the warmth and the greening of the earth.

Alban Hefin (21st June, summer solstice) – at this festival the mead and the whisky would have been blessed as part of a great summer celebration.

Gwyl Awst (1st August) – a feast of harvest and thanks, blessing the bannock/bread that would feed the Celts through the winter months.

Alban Elfed (21st Sept., autumnal equinox) – this is the time of strengthening darkness and the feast of the Cailleach, who is welcomed rather than feared. She brings the cold depths of winter, and feasting in her honour was thought to ensure the survival of the Clan through the winter months.

THE MAGIC OF THE PAINTED PEOPLE

In the Highlands of Scotland there is a branch of Paganism that has been practiced for hundreds of years by the Highlanders. It is known as PectiWita, or Wita. The term originates from the Picts or Picti, meaning painted, which refers to the fact that these people would paint themselves with blue dye from a woad plant. This was illustrated in the film 'Braveheart', although William Wallace actually lived much later than the Picts and it is unlikely that he painted his face blue to meet King Edward on the battlefield.

The Picts were a Celtic tribal people from the late Iron Age, who believed in being true to themselves, defending their territory valiantly and upholding a sense of freedom. This sense of freedom still resonates throughout Scotland today, and the Scots have a very tolerant 'live and let live' attitude to others.

PectiWita utilises aspects of traditional Highland dress, such as swords, sporrans, dirks and targes, as magical tools. I use a dirk, a type of dagger, as a substitute for the traditional witch's athame, and I find that it works just as well, lending a touch of PectiWita to my rituals and connecting me to my Bruce ancestors.

PRACTISING CELTIC MAGIC

As you can see from this chapter, Celtic magic is very similar to modern Wicca, and there might be much that already seems familiar to you or that resonates with you. The main tools used are a dirk, or some kind of blade, and a cauldron for holding fire spells, water etc. As a form of folk magic, however, Celtic magic relies mostly upon the inner power of the soul, of courage, forbearance and connection with nature. Throughout the rest of this book there will be spells, rituals, invocations and divinations for you to try so that you can connect with the magic of the Celts whenever you choose.

Chapter Three

CELTIC DEITIES

The Celts believed in a wide range of gods and goddesses. Some of these deities were worshipped in several Celtic regions, for example the Morrigan, who was held in high esteem throughout Scotland, Ireland and Wales. Others were central to a particular region, like Bran the Blessed, one of the Welsh gods. Still others were known by different names in different regions but are essentially the same deity. In this chapter we will look at some of the main deities of the Celtic pantheon and how they can be invoked for magical purposes.

Cernunnos is guardian of wildwoods.

CERNUNNOS: HORNED ONE

Cernunnos is probably the most important Celtic deity there is. A powerful god of forest and animals, he is depicted with antlers growing from his brow. He is seen as the guardian of wildlife and wildwood places. He has been worshipped for thousands of years, his image carved in rock, stone and iron by our primitive ancestors. Perhaps the most famous depiction of Cernunnos is the one on the Gundestrup cauldron, which dates from approximately 150BC – 1BC. This cauldron is a symbol of transformation and regeneration, representing the life cycle of birth, death and rebirth. In terms of magic, Cernunnos is a great all-rounder and he can be invoked for strength, courage, resilience, fertility, passion and protection. In England he was later known as Herne the Hunter. You can connect with him by spending time with deer, observing them in the Highlands or a deer park. Antlers are naturally shed each year, so adding one to your altar would honour this god. Invoke him with this traditional chant:

Hoof and horn, hoof and horn

All that dies shall be reborn

Cernunnos, Horned One

Guide my steps till day is done.

The Gundestrup cauldron famously depicts Cernunnos.

ARAWN: LORD OF ANNWN

Bearing some resemblance to Cernunnos is Arawn, the Welsh god of Annwn or the Otherworld. He is sometimes depicted with a pair of rams' horns spiralling from his head rather than antlers and, occasionally, with a skull's face to denote his role as Lord of Death. However, this shouldn't make him a fearsome god, for Arawn promises the blessing of an afterlife in Annwn, a land of abundant feasts and eternal happiness. Like Herne, Arawn is a Hunter god, often shown on horseback with a pack of hounds beside him. He is also known as Gwyn ap Nudd and, in this aspect, he is said to preside over the fairy realms and fairy portals. Magically, he can help you to attune with Elphame or the fairy realms, come to terms with a loss or bereavement, or prepare for the end of something. He is the strength in the sorrow, the hope of a new start following a loss. He should not be feared, but embraced, as he provides the life lessons that we all must learn. Arawn is associated with the season of autumn, as the natural world begins to die back, so attune with him by wearing autumnal colours, walking in the woods, or blowing a hunting horn or wind instrument. Invoke him with this chant:

Arawn, Arawn of spiralled horn

Of portals fair 'tween dark and dawn

Guide me through each loss I bear

I lean on you, your strength to share.

Arawn is also known as Gwyn ap Nudd and, in this aspect, presides over the fairy realms.

THE MORRIGAN: BATTLE GODDESS

The Morrigan is probably the most well-known of the Celtic goddesses. She was worshipped throughout the British Isles, particularly in Scotland and Ireland. Her Welsh counterpart is called Branwen, sister of Bran the Blessed. The Morrigan is a powerful Triple Goddess. Also known as The Three in One, she shapeshifts from maiden to mother to crone and back again, depending on the circumstances. She is, by turns, a seductive woman, a wise crone, and a mother figure who is all nurturing and giving. She is always a powerful source of protection. As a battle goddess, the Morrigan decides who lives and dies on the battlefield, and she is particularly drawn to warriors and the military. All members of the crow family are her sacred birds, so ravens, rooks, crows, magpies etc. are her messengers. Should any of these birds nest in your garden, it is said to mean that the Morrigan herself is watching over your household. However, it is bad luck to feed her carrion birds, and doing so can bring about misfortune. Collecting their naturally shed feathers, however, is a great way to connect with this goddess. She can help with disputes, unfair treatment, abuse, justice, victory and so on.

The Morrigan has a triple aspect and is often depicted as a crow.

Bear in mind that she has little time for troublemakers, so if the fault lies with you, the Morrigan will see justice served.

To cast a simple spell for her assistance, hold a black crow's feather in your hand and focus on your intention. So, for example, you might ask for the protection of your family or property. Hold the intention clearly in your mind, speak it out loud and invoke the Morrigan's assistance with this invocation, then let the feather fly on the wind:

Morrigan, I call you, hear my plight

By crow's feather taking flight

What is yours I return to thee

I ask your assistance, so mote it be.

CERRIDWEN: CAULDRON KEEPER

Cerridwen is a crone goddess and was very popular throughout Wales and Ireland. She is the keeper of the cauldron of transformation, and it is said that Celtic warriors would be taken into her cauldron in death, to be reborn in the afterlife or resurrected completely. In modern magic, the cauldron is still seen as a tool of transformation, with witches burning written spells in a cauldron to bring about manifestation of the magical goal. Cerridwen is the goddess of inspiration, transformation and transcendence. She encourages growth, expansion and learning, but with the caveat that with growth comes change. For a new phase of life to begin, an old one must end. You must be prepared to make sacrifices to experience transformation. Call on Cerridwen to help you with any period of change, for inspiration, growth, renewal or transformation of your life. Do this by writing your goal on a slip of paper and burning it in a small cauldron as you say:

Cerridwen, cauldron keeper

Take this desire true

Transform it in your cauldron

Make all that was renew

Cerridwen's cauldron continues to be a main tool for the modern witch.

The Bridestones rock formation in Todmorden, Yorkshire, is believed to have been named for the goddess Brigantia.

BRIGHID: LIGHT BEARER

Brighid is the Irish goddess of hearth and home. Also known as Bride, Bridget and Brigantia, she is the sacred flame of the hearthside, the heart of family life. As a goddess of spring, she brings the light back after a long winter, and the sabbat of Gwyn Forwyn is her sacred festival. Brighid is also a patron of poets, writers, bards and singers. Her energy is light, bright, loving and joyful. Invite her into your home by making a space for her, traditionally called Bride's Bed. Place a small chair, stool or cushion by the hearth – or the warmest spot in the house – and say:

Blessed Brighid I welcome you

Keep safe this hearth and home

Let your sacred fire burn

That none shall feel the cold

Welcome Bride!

BRAN AND BRANWEN

Bran, meaning raven, is a sun god in the Celtic pantheon, while his sister Branwen represented the moon. Both these deities feature strongly in Welsh folklore. When Branwen was mistreated by her husband, the king of Ireland, Bran exacted revenge in a great battle. There he rescued his sister, but he was struck with a poisoned dart during the battle. He gave orders that his head was to be removed and buried at the site that is now the Tower of London, where his sacred ravens still reside. Bran is a symbol of wisdom, prophetic dreams and augury, while Branwen represents resilience, forbearance, and courage in adversity. Together they are the epitome of family bonds and support, so invoke their aid with this chant if you need to increase your personal support system:

Bran the blessed and Branwen strong

Shape and form my family bonds

Stick together through thick and thin

As a family, we will win.

Bran means raven and is a sun god in the Celtic pantheon, with his sister Branwen representing the moon.

Aenghus is a god of love, and can transform himself into a swan.

AENGHUS: SWAN LORD

Aenghus (Angus) is a god of love. In Wales he was known as Mabon, after whom the autumnal sabbat in Wicca is named. His festival is the sabbat of Gwyl Awst in Celtic magic. Aenghus is a gentle god of romance, love, healing and water. He is said to guard the watery portals to the Otherworld, and he can transform himself into a swan in order to move among humans undetected. Like the swan, he is a symbol of pure, lasting love and successful partnerships. All water birds are under his protection, but swans and swan feathers are a sign that he is close by, casting his love magic on unsuspecting mortals! To invoke the romantic powers of this god, kiss a swan feather, then keep it close to your heart and say:

Swan love, pure love, lasting embrace

I dream of the Swan Prince, his strength and his grace

Calling sweet Aenghus, god of romance

Send me a lover for life's longest dance!

EPONA: HORSE GODDESS

Epona, or Rhiannon as she was known in Wales, is a goddess of horses, fertility, travel and liberty. As you would expect, all equines are sacred to this goddess and the Celts very much depended on their mounts, so it is natural that they should have worshipped a horse goddess. The chalk horses carved into hillsides in England could be a remnant of this kind of worship. Sometimes depicted as a horse, at other times shown as a rider, the goddess Epona was so important in Britain that the Romans actually adopted her as one of their own goddesses. In her darker aspect she is the fearsome Nightmare, who forces you to face your fears as you sleep. Sleep is one of her teaching tools, and dreams are how this goddess communicates. To attune with her, spend time with horses, go riding, give to an equine charity or help out at a stables.

A depiction of the goddess Epona riding a horse.

Being around horses can be very therapeutic. They are a symbol of freedom, travel and liberty. To bring the energies of this goddess into your life, find a lucky horseshoe for your altar and chant:

Epona, Epona teach me to ride

A life of adventure from which I won't hide

Obstacles cleared, the past left behind

As I go on this journey my fate now to find.

STUDY CELTIC MYTHOLOGY

These are just a few of the Celtic deities. There are many, many more. Studying the mythology of the Celts will introduce you to more gods and goddesses that you might choose to work with. Remember to hold your intention firmly in your head and heart as you request a deity's assistance. You can invoke these gods and goddesses to make your life run more smoothly and to give you a magical edge. Just remember to always be respectful, do your research when working with new deities, and find different ways to connect with them that work for you.

Chapter Four

KINGS AND QUEENS

In Britain we have a long history of monarchy. Right from the earliest Celtic queens and the famous battles of Medieval kings, we have a very regal past. Some of these royal figures have become legendary icons, and people still admire and talk about them centuries later.

The statue of Boudicca and her daughters in London.

TWO QUEENS, ONE PROBLEM

When the Romans invaded Britain, the Celts faced a difficult dilemma: live in peace, but under Roman rule, with the possibility of being forced into slavery and made to fight Roman wars; or fight the Romans to try and maintain control of their own island and their tribal way of life. Two Celtic queens handled this dilemma in very different ways.

Boudicca was queen of the Iceni tribe. After the death of her husband, the Romans, being a patriarchal society, refused to recognise her as queen and came to take over her lands. When Boudicca refused to give up her royal claim and homelands, the Romans flogged her for disobedience and raped both her daughters, mistakenly believing that this would bring Boudicca to heel. It didn't. It roused her rebel heart and she took revenge on the Romans by leading an army of Iceni and Trinovante warriors and sacking the city of Camulodunum, which is modern-day Colchester. From there she moved on to Londinium (London), where she repeated the victory. Ultimately, though, Boudicca was defeated, and disappeared from history. Some say that she died of her injuries or illness, while others claim that she took poison so as not to live under Roman rule. Whatever the truth may be, she certainly gave the Romans a sting they didn't forget, and in documenting her name and victories, they left behind her legacy of rebellion to be pored over by scholars and historians for years to come. Centuries later, we still say her name with admiration, and Boudicca has become a legendary figure, striding though history, standing against oppression. Today, a statue commemorating her courageous victory stands in London, near Westminster Bridge.

Further north, Cartimandua, queen of the Brigantes, took a very different tactic when it came to the Romans. She became their ally. Cartimandua believed that the best way to ensure the survival of her tribe was to merge it with the new governing force via trade and a common understanding. In this way, she hoped to maintain some control over her lands and her people. The tactic worked for some time, and the Brigantes and Romans seemed to co-exist quite successfully – until Cartimandua divorced her husband, which led to him arranging a rebellion against both Cartimandua *and* the Romans. While the rebellion failed the first time, the second one was more successful, and Cartimandua had to be rescued by Roman soldiers. At this point she disappeared from history, and no-one knows what happened to her, but her decision to ally with the Romans made the Brigantes one of the wealthiest, most successful tribes in ancient Britain.

Both these queens demonstrate that a sense of freedom was, and still is, incredibly important to the Celts. While Boudicca and Cartimandua had different tactics for dealing with Roman invasion, they both had the same goal, which was to maintain a sense of autonomy and control over their own destiny and that of their people.

Boudicca Spell to Stand Against Oppression

On the night of the full moon, take a black candle and carve into the wax the nature of the oppression you are facing. This could be racism, bigotry, workplace bullying, sexism, harassment etc. On the other side of the candle carve Boudicca's name. Hold the candle in your hands and picture Boudicca fighting the Romans from her war chariot. Now change the visualisation so that you are standing in the chariot, defeating those who oppress you, with Boudicca by your side. When you can see this image clearly in your mind, light the candle and say the following chant three times, then allow the candle to burn down. Repeat the spell each full moon until the oppression stops. Wear her hare totem for extra connection.

I call on Boudicca, Iceni Queen

To strengthen my resolve

I am not alone, she fights with me

Oppression is now dissolved

From her chariot I will fight

Her valour helps me shine

Those who target me now take flight

For victory is mine!

So mote it be.

Cartimandua Spell for Negotiation

Sometimes you have to ask for what you want. Take a tip from Cartimandua and negotiate your way to a better deal. This spell could be used before a job interview, or a meeting to discuss a promotion or a pay increase. If you are buying a big-ticket item, such as a new car, cast this spell to ensure you get a good deal. Take two slips of paper and on each one write the positive outcome you are going to negotiate for, say a pay increase, or better working hours etc. Hold them both to your heart and say:

Cartimandua, Brigantes Queen

I summon your skills from beyond the Unseen

Help me negotiate a better deal

Speak with my voice to make my goal real

Lend me your wisdom, your ruthless drive

To take on the challenge and ensure that I thrive.

So mote it be.

Burn one slip of paper in your cauldron, sending your goal out into the universe, and keep the other with you until you have negotiated your new reality. Good luck!

SCATHACH: WARRIOR QUEEN

Far to the north, on the Isle of Skye, lived the Celtic queen Scathach, pronounced Skaaha. Although a Scots queen of the Highlands, Islands and Caledonii regions, she was strongly allied with the Irish tribes as well. Her fortress of Dun Scaith on Skye was long since built over, and it is now the ruins of Dun Sgathgaich. It was here that both Scots and Irish warriors would be sent for training, because Scathach was far more than a simple queen – she was a warrior queen who trained the elite soldiers of her time. Young men would have to scale the walls of her fortress to prove that they were worthy of her training.

Scathach was a battle queen, skilled in all the arts of war, from strategy and negotiation to physical combat with sword, spear and hand-to-hand grappling, or what we would now refer to as martial arts. The fact that her name means *Shadowy One* would also indicate that she had skills in infiltration, extraction and assassination. She was not a queen to be messed with!

Scathach is perhaps most famous for training Cuchullain, also known as the Warrior of Ulster, who eventually became her champion.

Skilled in the martial arts, Queen Scathach famously trained the warriors of Scotland and Ireland.

It is thought that she had a romantic relationship with him too, but he later betrayed her with another woman, for which she banished him from Skye. Still, to this day, the island bears his name in the form of the Cuillin mountains, so his influence lingers on.

The relationship between Scathach and Cuchullain is one of the most complex and romantic in Celtic folklore. While the Irish continue to tell stories of their great Ulster hero, in the Scottish Highlands and Islands, it is his tutor, Scathach, who holds all the glory and who is recounted with admiration.

Scathach Spell to Get Over a Betrayal

B eing betrayed by someone you love and trust is one of the most devastating experiences. It can leave you feeling lost, cut adrift, as if everything you thought you knew is a lie. It robs you of the future you once envisioned. Whether the betrayal comes from a lover, a best friend or a co-worker, betrayal of any kind hits hard and leaves a deep wound. Use this spell invoking Scathach to help you to move through the pain and into peace of mind.

Take a sheet of paper and cut it into a heart shape. On the heart write the nature of the betrayal in red pen. Allow yourself to feel whatever comes up for you as you do this. Take your time with it, holding the heart and absorbing what this betrayal now means for your future.

When you feel ready, invoke Scathach's strength of will, to help banish the traitor from your life and your heart.

Scathach, queen of Skye

Betrayed is my heart, blinded my eyes

Now I see what once was hidden

Through lies and deceit the truth was bidden

Give me strength to heal my heart

To fight this war as trust departs

Banish the traitor, get them gone

Free me at last, to start moving on

So mote it be.

Tear the heart to shreds and add the pieces to a fire or scatter them to the four winds, for closure.

Triple Queens Protection Spell

I f you ever feel yourself under threat or in an unsafe situation, call on all three ancient queens of the Celts for their protection, by saying the following invocation:

Boudicca, Cartimandua, Scathach, Circle round

Guard and protect me from all harm around!

Keep me safe wherever I roam

Guide my steps, lead me home.

So mote it be.

ROBERT THE BRUCE: KING OF SCOTS

Ask anyone in Scotland who The Good King is and they'll say Robert the Bruce. Robert I was King of Scots from 1306 to 1329, but his claim to the crown was not without dispute and his road to the throne was

A carving of Robert the Bruce in a Scottish forest.

rocky, to say the least! When King Alexander III died after a fall from his horse in 1286, and his successor, the Maid of Norway, drowned on her way to claim the throne, the crown of Scotland was up for grabs. Edward I, King of England, quickly claimed overlordship of Scotland. This didn't go down well with the Scots, and years of bloody battles followed as the Scots tried to reclaim their country.

Robert the Bruce had a strong claim to the crown, but there was also another claimant – John Comyn, from the powerful Clan Comyn, which held vast swathes of the Highlands. The two men agreed to meet at Greyfriars Kirk in Dumfries, to discuss the best way forward, but an argument ensued and the Bruce killed his rival. From then on it was a race to get crowned and accepted as King of Scots. The Scottish church backed his claim, but Clan Comyn were understandably set against him – inciting a rivalry and blood feud that continues to this day. After many skirmishes, the Bruce eventually won his crown, ultimately sealing his place as king with his great victory at the battle of Bannockburn in 1314.

None of this would have been possible if the Bruce hadn't followed his ambition. He made mistakes along the way and deeply regretted killing Comyn, but his years on the throne led to a more prosperous and independent Scotland, free from English rule. For that he will always be known as *The Good King*.

THE REBEL HEART

If there is one thing that the Celts are known for, Robert the Bruce included, it is their rebel hearts! In Celtic culture having a rebel heart is no bad thing. It depends entirely on how it is used. The rebel heart is just as important as the warrior spirit, and the two frequently go hand in hand.

I would go further and say that the rebel heart is vital to facilitate positive change. Without the rebel heart, abusers would never be challenged, dictators would never be toppled, and corrupt governments and organisations would continue to rule supreme. In such situations we need a certain amount of rebellion, for it is the catalyst to freedom.

Yes, rebellion can be messy and sacrifices have to be made, but on the other side of it usually lies peace and freedom, so it is a battle worth fighting.

Robert the Bruce believed so strongly that his men would follow wherever his heart led them, that he gave orders for his heart to be cut from his body upon his death and carried in a casket to the Holy Land, where his men were to fight on Crusade without him. His heart and his body are buried in two separate places in Scotland, his body in Dunfermline and his heart in Melrose. This is the reason he is known as the original braveheart.

Rouse the Rebel Heart Spell

Y ou can nurture your own rebel heart to increase your courage and to help you stand up to people who try to bully you, control you or renege on agreements. Simply take a symbol of a heart – a pendant, crystal, stone or a heart cut from card – and hold it to your own heart, saying the following incantation:

With warrior spirit I play my part

I nurture within my rebel heart

I won't be controlled

I was born to be free

My rebellious heart they now shall see!

MARY, QUEEN OF SCOTS: THE CAPTIVE QUEEN

One of Scotland's most romantic figures, Mary, Queen of Scots was the disputed successor to the English throne, plotting against Elizabeth I.

Born in Stirling in 1542, she spent her early years in Scotland before being betrothed to the Dauphin of France and moving to the French court. She was the Queen of France from 1559 until her husband's death in 1560, when she returned to Scotland to take up her rule there, but she was plagued by rebellious Scots who would not be ruled by a woman. This is ironic, to say the least, coming from a region in which Queen Scathach once trained male warriors!

In 1568, Mary made the mistake of fleeing to England, seeking shelter and support against her Scots enemies. Instead she was imprisoned as a 'royal guest' of Elizabeth I. Mary was moved from one English castle to another to ensure that no rescue attempt was ever successful. All in all, she spent over eighteen years in captivity. In 1586 she became embroiled in the infamous Babington Plot to assassinate Queen Elizabeth and take the English throne, and for this she was finally executed. She was beheaded for treason at Fotheringhay Castle in 1587.

For all her romance, Mary is also a rather tragic figure, for she was largely used as a pawn in the political intrigues of powerful men. Married three times and crowned twice, yet it could be argued that she never knew a day of security or real autonomy in her life. Her ambitions served her ill, and her recklessness in plotting the death of Elizabeth I led to her downfall. It is said that Elizabeth had no desire to kill her cousin and her hand was forced by Mary's actions. Mary had taken an unnecessary risk, and lost.

Spell to Avoid Unnecessary Risks

Y ou will need a tealight and holder for this simple spell. Hold the tealight in your hands and repeat the incantation three times, then light it in the holder and allow it to burn down. Use this spell whenever you feel tempted to be reckless or to take unnecessary risks:

Overzealous I will not be

No captive to my schemes

I will not over-reach my plans

I know the limit to my dreams!

Chapter Five

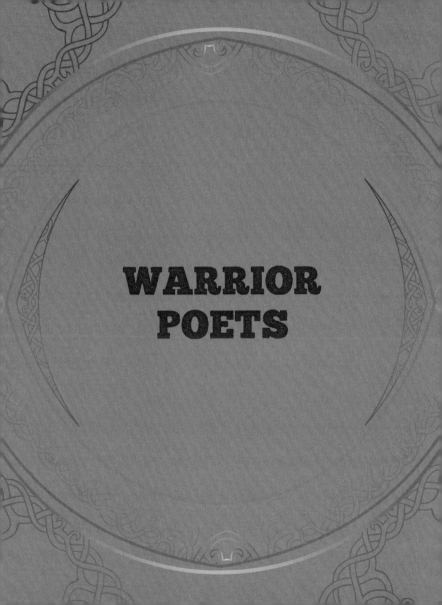

WARRIOR POETS

For the Celts, war was a way of life. They fought to hold territory; they had skirmishes in clan disputes and they battled for the greater wealth and provision of their people. Battle was as much a part of the Celtic lifestyle as tilling the fields or raising a flock of sheep. Young men had to be always battle-ready, in case the clan chief or local laird called them to arms. The women needed to be ready to tend wounds and lay out the fallen. Even the children would have been expected to help out, as squires, drummers or water-bearers. War was in their DNA.

But the Celts were far more than just petty scrappers or freedom fighters. They were warrior poets. This is a term coined in Scottish and Irish folklore. Put simply, it refers to one who fights for a higher purpose or for a greater good. Warrior poets were idealistic soldiers who fought with a strong moral compass. The idea of committing war crimes would be abhorrent to them, likewise the *'raising of the red dragon'* (not to be confused with the Welsh flag!), which was a banner from Mediaeval times meaning that no mercy would be shown and all enemy forces on the battlefield would be slaughtered, whether they tried to surrender or not. Edward I raised the red dragon against the

Scots more than once, so determined was he to crush them. It didn't work, as you will see later in this chapter.

A warrior poet fought with mind, body and spirit. He was a holistic soldier. Brutal force wasn't all that made up a Celtic warrior. In addition to battle skills, he would have developed a strategic mind and he would have held in his heart the reason he was fighting, be that for his clan, his country or his honour. Honour was hugely important among the Celts. They gave their word and kept it, considering any double dealing or deceit to be cowardly and a sign of weakness.

The warrior poet was motivated by love and compassion, not glory or brutality. If battle came, he would face it with courage, but he didn't go out looking for trouble. He would fight to protect his own, considering it an honour to protect his clan and his loved ones. He was an intelligent warrior, as well as an instinctive one.

In later years, the warrior poets began to document their thoughts and deeds on the battlefield. This gave rise to what we now term The War Poets and much of what we know of the trenches of the first and second world wars derives from the words written by the warrior poets of the time. This is just one of the ways in which Celtic culture is still prevalent in modern history.

BECOMING A WARRIOR POET

We all face troubles from time to time and occasionally we might need to fight our own corner and do battle to defend our rights. Too often, though, we go in with a knee-jerk reaction, when we should take a breath and make a calculated response instead. This difference between an unfettered temper tantrum and a more considered response, is what separates a bully from a warrior.

Warriors need not shout, while bullies are full of bravado. Warriors have the ability to control their aggression, while bullies are fuelled by their temper and have little to no control. Warriors know when to attack, mediate, negotiate, placate or fall back. Bullies only know how to attack. Warriors will defend those weaker than themselves, while a bully will target them.

So how do you become more of a warrior poet in your own life? First, take full responsibility for your thoughts, words and deeds. If you make a mistake, own up to it. You're only human and mistakes are allowed. Don't participate in gossip or bullying of any kind – in fact, stand against it, calmly. Be kind. Be helpful to those who might need a hand. Be considerate and show compassion to others.

If someone attacks you in some way, be it a bullying boss or a catty colleague, stand up to them. Literally. Stand up, speak firmly without raising your voice and tell them that you won't be treated that

way. What we allow, we condone, and we *teach* people how they can treat us. This means that you should never put up with ill-treatment, bullying or controlling behaviour from anyone. Regain your autonomy by standing up for yourself. In this way you will develop the strength of character to face adversity when it comes your way.

Finally, if you do find yourself in a conflict of some kind, breathe deeply before you make your response. Give yourself time to think and to calculate the risks. Then say your piece calmly and firmly, and simply walk away, leaving them to digest your response. If you have done a good job, there should be no need for further engagement. Sadly, conflict is a fact of life. Inevitably you will experience it at some point. When you do, approach it as a warrior poet, with a strong moral compass and compassion for your enemy and you won't go far wrong.

Creating a Battle Plan for Life

The Celts were great strategists. They knew exactly what they wanted from any conflict or negotiation. Holding the end point in mind is essential in any victory, because otherwise how will you know when you have won? You don't want to go on fighting, way past the point where you had exactly what you were fighting for, because that way you will only exhaust yourself. You must know exactly what victory or success looks like to you, so that you can recognise when you have reached that point and take a well-earned break.

This is as true for life as it is for warfare. The truth is that life will feel like less of a battleground if you approach it with a strategy in place. Those people who drift through life with no goals, no ambitions and no direction are usually the ones who end up most dissatisfied, unfulfilled, miserable and envious of others.

Take charge of your future by formulating a strategic battle plan. This will help you to keep on track with your goals and get you to where you want to be. Achievement is an important life-skill to master because it leads to greater personal confidence. The more confidence you have, the more open you will be to new experiences and opportunities. Once you have ticked off most of your goals, make a new battle plan to keep your life moving forward.

THE BATTLE PLAN

Take a large sheet of paper and divide it into three equal sections, and title each section so:

Short-Term Goals: 0–6 months

Mid-Term Goals: 6 months–2 years

Long-Term Goals: 2–5 years

Next, begin to fill out each section. List all the things that you want to achieve in the next six months. Make sure these goals are realistic for the time frame you are working with. If they're not achievable in six months, put them in one of the other sections. Try to have a mixture of personal, career and hobby goals so that you are improving your life-balance as you go. Once you have filled out the first section, move onto the next two sections. When you have your battle plan all figured out, you effectively have the next five years of your life mapped out on paper. Each time you achieve a goal, tick it off.

Keep your Battle Plan in a safe place, perhaps on your altar. Once you have written it all out, roll it up like a scroll and bless it by passing it through incense smoke as you say:

I feel the need to press ahead

To make my dreams come true

As I make my goals reality

My life is shaped anew

I learn from my ancestors

To hold my battle ground

I create my own sense of victory

To my own success I'm bound.

Notable Warrior Poets

William Wallace – Quite possibly the most famous Celtic freedom fighter in the UK, if not the world, Wallace successfully routed Edward I's much larger army at the Battle of Stirling Bridge in 1297. He stirred up the Scots to stand against the oppression of English occupation, until he was betrayed and captured by Sir John Menteith and taken to London, where he was executed in 1305. He is still Scotland's national hero and a global icon for freedom and independence.

Isabella MacDuff, Countess of Buchan – Isabella is a great heroine of Scotland because she defied her Comyn husband and rode out to crown his rival, Robert the Bruce, King of Scots! This was an ancient right of the Earls of Fife, but with her brother, who was Earl at that time, imprisoned in England, Isabella took it upon herself to honour this tradition. For her boldness and bravery, she was harshly punished, being confined to live in a cage hung on the outside of Berwick castle.

Rob Roy Macgregor – Rob Roy was a Jacobite who fought in support of the exiled Stuart King James. He was known for both protecting and raiding cattle, for which he was branded an outlaw. He fought at the Jacobite Uprising of 1715 and died in 1734. He is buried at Balquidder, near his home on Loch Lomond, with his wife Mary and two of their sons. He will always be known as a Child of the Mists and Macgregor Despite Them.

Llywelyn ap Gruffudd – Son of Llywelyn the Great, Llywelyn ap Gruffudd is known as the Last Prince of Wales, from 1258-82. That is, he was the very last sovereign and Welsh-born Prince of Wales. Llywelyn refused to pay homage to King Edward I and was a key figure in the rebellion against him. He was therefore declared a rebel, much like William Wallace. His family were allies of Clan Comyn in the Highlands of Scotland. Upon Llywelyn's death, Edward named his son, the future Edward II, Prince of Wales as a symbol of his conquest of Wales.

Toasting the Water

Toasting the water is a common practice in Scotland and it can easily be incorporated into your magical rituals. Simply pass the ritual chalice of wine, or a glass of whisky as is more traditional, over a jug or cauldron of water and make a toast or a wish before drinking. You can use a chalice of juice or water if you don't drink.

This tradition is associated with the Jacobites, the supporters of the Stuart Kings in the 18th century, of which Rob Roy was one – and he would have indulged in this tradition himself. To keep their support a secret, they would silently toast their leader, who was in exile across the water in France. This was a good way for Jacobites to show their allegiance and to recognise one another. It is said that the practice has its origins in ancient Pictish magic, but it is still performed today by Scots all over the world, as a toast to their ancestral roots. Before you drink say *"Slainte mhath!"*(pronounced slanj-a-va), which is a Gaelic toast to good health.

Braveheart Spell for Adventure

I f you ever feel trapped, caged or hemmed in, this spell can help you to take back your autonomy and rouse your spirit of adventure! Take a golden candle for new opportunities and carve the words Braveheart and Adventure down the length of it. Light the candle and chant the incantation below three times, then let the candle burn down.

Razzle, dazzle flying free

The spirit of adventure carries me

From a mundane cage I now depart

I unleash my power as a true braveheart!

Chapter Six

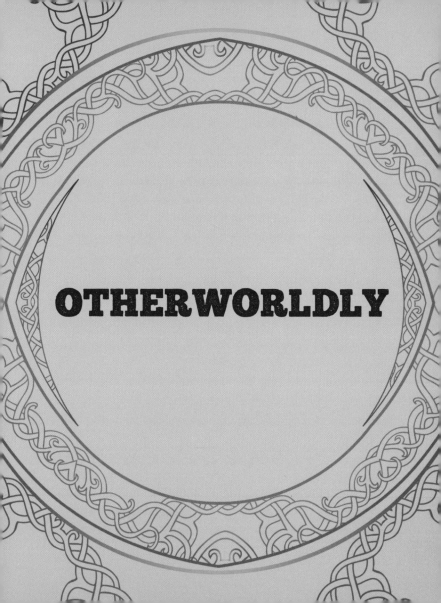

OTHERWORLDLY

C eltic culture is full of superstition and folklore, which should come as no surprise given that the Celts are a storytelling community. While many of their folkloric beings were originally thought to be a benevolent force, with the rise of Christianity came the demonization of the Celtic fey. As you will see, many of these folkloric spirits are now linked with death or are considered to be bad omens, yet originally they were simply messengers from the Otherworld, with magical powers and gifts to share with those who were fortunate enough to see them. Do bear this in mind as you read about these magical beings.

THE CAILLEACH: BLUE HAG OF WINTER

The Cailleach is the Celtic goddess of winter. She is occasionally depicted as a seductive young ice-maiden, but more usually as an old woman with blue-tinged skin. She brings the cold season and sprinkles the mountains with snow. She makes the world over with frost, ice and snowflakes. The Cailleach wants people to enjoy the gifts of her season, to enjoy a cold, frosty walk or skiing in the mountains, before returning home to a warm hearthside and a hearty bowl of soup. She protects those who welcome her and her season, but she can be something of a trickster to those who moan about the winter weather, causing slips and falls and all manner of winter problems.

As a spirit of winter, she should be welcomed at the time of the autumnal equinox or Samhain at the latest, with the house made ready

The Cailleach brings frost, ice and snowflakes to the world in winter.

for the colder months to come. Preparing for the winter is a good way to honour this deity and to keep on her good side as it shows a healthy, mindful respect for the cold weather, so feel free to light a winter-scented candle in honour of the Cailleach as you go about hanging warmer curtains, laying down thick rugs or even chopping wood for the wood-burner if you have one. Fill up the freezer with goodies, stock up on candles and buy any new winter clothes you need. Make sure your winter sports gear, such as ice skates, are in good condition and see to any repairs that need doing before the dark of winter really sets in. The Cailleach will appreciate all such preparations for her season.

In Scotland they say "The Cailleach is on you" if someone is suffering from the effects of the cold and showing signs of hypothermia. Their skin will take on a blue tinge, just like the Blue Hag herself, and they will feel numb and very sleepy, showing symptoms of extreme shivering and teeth chattering as they begin to warm up. When the Cailleach is on you, heed her warning and retreat indoors, have a hot drink and allow yourself to warm up gradually, by a crackling fireside.

The Cailleach isn't malevolent. She is simply winter, and she must be respected as such, for winter can be a dangerous time. Enjoy her season, but err on the side of caution by casting this spell for her protection before you venture out into the cold for any length of time.

Cailleach Spell for a Safe Winter

Y ou will need a blue lace agate crystal, or a token that represents the wintertime, such as a snowflake brooch or necklace. On the night when the clocks go back and British Summer Time ends, or a dark night in your time zone, light a tealight and place it into a lantern. Take this outside, along with your winter token, and sit for moment, breathing in the dark, autumnal air. Know that from now on the days will become visibly shorter and the nights longer, colder and darker. Hold your winter token in your hands, look up at the sky and say:

I welcome the Cailleach, I welcome the Blue Hag

I ask her protection as the sky rains black

I call on the Cailleach to watch over us all

To see us through winter and every snowfall

I honour the Cailleach with this glowing flame

I welcome the winter in her name

As I enjoy all her gifts of winter's delight

I ask her protection, from now till Spring's light.

Protecting us all with warmth, wealth and good cheer

As we feast with our family throughout the next year!

So mote it be.

Leave the lantern outside until the tealight has burnt itself out. Put the crystal or token into your winter coat pocket, or wear it, so that you carry it with you throughout the winter months. If you want, you can cast this spell with several crystals or tokens, one for each family member, to keep them safe through the snowy season of winter.

WASHER AT THE FORD

The Washer, or ban nighe, is another form of hag spirit and is thought by some to be an aspect of the Cailleach. Similar to the ban sidhe or banshee, to see the Washer at the Ford is an omen, even if it is only in a dream. She appears at the side of a loch or stream, washing a plaid. If the plaid is washed clean, it was a good omen, but if she washed blood from the plaid and the water turned red, it was a sign that someone close would die. The colours of the plaid were also significant, as this would foretell which clan the omen referred to. If she was washing sheets stained with blood, this meant a death in childbirth, be it mother or babe. Originally, the Washer at the Ford would grant three wishes to those who saw her and spoke to her unafraid, but the rise of Christianity dissolved this aspect of the superstition and made the Washer a harbinger of death. In her aspect as a water spirit, her role was to guard the water she was linked to, and libations of whisky, cider or beer would be poured into the water to keep this spirit benevolent and ward off her bad omens.

THE WILD HUNT

Probably one of the spookiest aspects of Celtic folklore, the Wild Hunt is well known in various mythologies, including Scottish, Irish, Welsh and Norse. As the name suggests, the Wild Hunt is a hunting party, but one that you would not wish to saddle up for! It is a spectral Hunt, led by a phantom Horseman, with a pack of ghostly hounds running alongside his midnight-black mount. Legend states that both horse and hounds have glowing red eyes and foaming mouths, while the Horseman is hooded – or headless!

To see or hear the Wild Hunt has long been considered a bad omen and, although it can be encountered at any time of year, it is more usual for this legend to resurface during the dark autumn and winter months. The Wild Hunt rides in on the billowing clouds of a storm-filled sky. The eerie sound of the hunting horn blows in on the wind, trumpeting through the treetops. The Wild Hunt's purpose is to gather up the souls of the dead and carry them away to the Otherworld.

The Horseman who leads the Hunt is by turns Arawn, Cernunnos, Herne the Hunter, Gwyn ap Nudd or Odin, depending on the region and culture. In Ireland he is associated with Dullachan, a headless horseman who wanders the byways looking for lost souls to take. Again, the Dullachan was said to be a harbinger of death. Even today, having dreams or nightmares of shadowy figures is linked with anxiety, worry, depression, despair and melancholia, so heed this message from your subconscious if you experience such dreams on a regular basis, and seek out help if you need it.

It is safe to say that Washington Irving was probably inspired by the folklore of the Wild Hunt when he wrote *The Legend of Sleepy Hollow*, and the Hunt remains a prevalent aspect of Celtic folklore. While you are unlikely to see the Hunt in full force, you might experience hints of it – in the shapes of storm clouds or the sound of the autumn wind blowing through the forests and hills. It was said that hiding in a kirk or church would protect one from the Hunt as it rode by, but avoid sheltering under yew trees, for they are portals through which the Huntsman rides, and you will put yourself directly in his path!

Protection from the Wild Hunt

To this day, it is considered a very bad omen if you should witness the Wild Hunt, so as it rides through the sky on stormy tides, it is always a good idea to say this simple protective incantation as you hear the storm coming in:

Wild Hunt, Storm Rider,

Pass by me and mine

Leave safe this house, no ill to bear

In your wake leave all benign.

THE MIRRIE DANCERS

On a much brighter note, the Mirrie Dancers are said to be an omen of good fortune, and to see them dancing is said to be very lucky indeed. Also known as Fox Fire, Northern Lights or the Aurora Borealis, the Mirrie Dancers have delighted onlookers all over the northern

The Mirrie Dancers over Callanish Stones.

hemisphere. Caused by atmospheric conditions, in the darkest winter nights the sky lights up with swirls of green and blue and golden light. It shimmers and dances through the sky, in a similar motion to starling murmurations in autumn. I have seen the Mirrie Dancers myself in the Scottish Highlands and it is the most magical experience. If you are lucky enough to see them, be sure to make a wish! As an alternative to travelling, view the Northern Lights online, then say this spell for added good fortune:

Mirrie Dancers shining bright

Fox Fire, bring your light

Fill my life with luck and charm

A love who keeps me safe from harm

Swirling, dancing through the night

Fire of gold and emerald bright

No matter where on earth I roam

I take with me the light of home.

Chapter Seven

HERALDIC
BEASTS
AND CELTIC
CREATURES

P ower animals or totems are an important aspect of Celtic magic. The Celts believed in a wide range of fantastical and mythical creatures, a few of which we will be looking at in this chapter. Some of those creatures took on prominent places in Celtic culture, for instance the red dragon in Wales or the unicorn in Scotland. Depicted on flags, shields, targes and carved in stone, animal totems stride through Celtic mythology and history, with some even maintaining their place of honour to this day. Working with them in magic is largely an exercise of visualisation, which means that no matter where you are or what you are doing, you always have access to these fabled creatures to give you a magical edge in your daily life.

THE UNICORN

One of the heraldic beasts of Scotland, and still present on the British coat of arms, the unicorn is a symbol of purity, liberty, freedom, chastity and virtue. In 15th- and 16th-century Scotland, it was a form of currency, with coins called Unicorns and Half-Unicorns in distribution. To this day, statues of the unicorn can be seen all over Scotland, from Inverness to Edinburgh, and along with the Red Lion Rampant, the unicorn holds up the Scottish flag in heraldic design.

Magically speaking, the unicorn is associated with the moon. Its spiralled horn, the alicorn, was said to be able to detect poison and purify water. In mythology it could not be held by chains or bars; it gallops so swiftly it could never be caught and was only captured by

Detail of the fountain in the inner courtyard of Linlithgow Palace in Scotland.

a maiden – that is a female virgin of virtuous intent. The unicorn is a universal symbol of magic, miracles, enchantment and innocence the world over. Although a gentle creature, it can also be ferocious when crossed, defending its liberty valiantly. Perhaps this is the reason the Scots took it as one of their heraldic beasts. It is certainly regarded as a very protective totem, and one that can inspire you towards greater independence. The unicorn is still known as one of the Queen's Beasts, and is associated with the current British monarchy.

Unicorn Spell for Independence

Cast this spell whenever you feel your independence and autonomy are being compromised. Take a picture or statue of a unicorn and place it on the altar before you. Place a pure white spiralled candle nearby in a suitable holder and light it. This represents the magical alicorn. Think about the ways in which your independence is being curtailed, then visualise a unicorn galloping towards you to carry you away into a life of greater liberty and freedom. Say this incantation nine times:

Sacred horse of equine grace

I call your spirit to this place

Bring your strength, protection and light

For my freedom I will fight

None shall take my liberty

As I ride with you, wild and free!

Allow the alicorn candle to burn down and take steps to increase your sense of independence and freedom.

How to Create an Alicorn Wand

Y ou can enhance your magic by using an alicorn wand. This is a wand that you have fashioned to represent the magical horn of a unicorn. You will need a stick of wood or dowelling, silver paint, silver or white glitter, glue, a white satin ribbon long enough to wrap around the stick, and a pointed aurora borealis crystal.

First paint the stick all over using the silver paint. While the paint is still tacky, roll the wand in silver or white glitter until it shimmers. (You can get biodegradable glitter now that isn't an environmental problem.) Once it has dried thoroughly, glue the crystal to one end to form the wand's tip, then wrap the ribbon clockwise around the wand in a spiral motion to give the wand an alicorn effect. Glue the ribbon in place as you go, paying particular attention to the ends. Allow the glue to dry, then bless the wand by passing it through incense smoke and saying:

Alicorn wand of enchantment and light

Shine unicorn magic, bring all that is bright

Add to my magic, lend unicorn charm

As I use this wand to enchant and disarm.

Use the alicorn wand to direct energy in your spells, just as you would use any other type of magical wand.

THE WATER KELPIE

In Scottish folklore the fearsome water kelpie is a malevolent water spirit that takes on the guise of a beautiful black or grey horse, grazing peacefully by the side of a loch. Its seemingly gentle nature is designed to draw in the unwary, for if one tries to pet the horse, or ride it, it will leap into the depths of the loch and drown its unfortunate rider. In some tales the water kelpie becomes a black unicorn and is an omen of death. It is afraid of iron,

A depiction of a water kelpie.

The Red Lion Rampant is a heraldic symbol in Scotland and appears on the Royal Standard flag.

being a fairy horse, so carrying a piece of iron, such as a nail, with you when travelling near lochs and burns is a wise precaution to take!

THE RED LION RAMPANT

The Red Lion Rampant is the second heraldic beast of Scotland and appears on the Royal Standard flag. It is a symbol of royalty, strength, power and protection. As the unicorn represents the moon, so the red lion represents the sun, and, magically speaking, these two heraldic beasts together represent duality and the balance of nature.

Long associated with the monarchs of Scotland, the Red Lion Rampant stands tall upon his hind legs, daring anyone to come closer to the claws of his posturing forepaws! He represents courage, bravery and boldness and is a symbol of sovereignty. Robert the Bruce would have fought beneath this banner, as would Mary, Queen of Scots. Although technically these days it can only be flown by Queen Elizabeth II at her royal palaces in Scotland, it is also widely sold as a souvenir. So you can *own* the Royal Standard, as I do, you just can't *fly* it! That said, you can still invoke the spirit of the Red Lion Rampant for magical purposes.

Red Lion Rampant Spell for Courage

I s there any creature more synonymous with courage than the lion? Probably not, which is why it is a popular heraldic beast. The Red Lion Rampant can remind you of your own strength and bolster your courage in adversity. For this spell, you will need some kind of image that represents the red lion of Scotland, be this a flag, a postcard or a print bought online. Alternatively, you can purchase lapel pins and jewellery from gifts shops in tourist spots across Scotland, or on their websites. Once you have your image, take it to your altar, light a red candle and think of all that the red lion represents. Think of Robert the Bruce fighting for his crown, or William Wallace fighting for independence. Think of the courage and bravery shown by all the people who have fought and gone into battle beneath the image of this beast over the centuries. Close your eyes and tap into this strength, for it belongs to you too. Feel your heart swell with the pride of the red lion, and then say these words:

I call the red lion of tooth and claw

Downtrodden I will be no more

For my faults I shall atone

Let courage now fill my flesh and bone

I Rally to the Red Lion, Scotland's Pride

Now let us do or let us die!

As those before me have fought and fell

I share their courage; all doubt I repel

I stand my ground with strength and valour

And bring forth my courage from this hour.

Allow the candle to burn down, and feel free to repeat this spell whenever you are facing adversity or a particular challenge. Invoke the courage of the red lion and claim it for your own.

THE WELSH DRAGON

Perhaps even older than the Red Lion Rampant is the Red Dragon of Wales, which is reputed to have been the royal standard of King Arthur himself. As their heraldic beast, the Red Dragon banner is

The Red Dragon of Wales is thought to be the royal standard of King Arthur.

flown all over Wales. In history, it was of course the banner of Henry Tudor, father of Henry VIII, and was the banner he fought under to win his victory over Richard III at the Battle of Bosworth Field. This Tudor influence is still seen in the white and green background of the Welsh Flag – white and green were the colours of the House of Tudor. To this day, the Red Dragon is known as one of the Queen's Beasts. It is a symbol of power, wisdom, sovereignty and survival.

How to Make Dragon's Breath Incense for Wisdom

For this spell you will need a mortar and pestle, a clean empty jar, a sticky label, a pen, and a selection of the following dried herbs: sage, mint, rosemary and basil. You will also need a loose incense burner and charcoal blocks.

Into the mortar place three tablespoons of each of the dried herbs. These herbs represent wisdom, clarity, protection and power. Grind them to a fine powder using the pestle. Once you have your blended incense, pour it into the jar and label it Dragon's Breath Incense. Hold the jar in your hands and empower it by saying:

Red Dragon of fiery might

Lend your wisdom, send your light

Celtic drake old and wise

May your breath filter truth from lies

Dragon's breath smoking free

Knowledge is power, so mote it be.

Whenever you have need for greater wisdom, clarity or concentration, light a charcoal block in your incense burner and add three pinches of dragon's breath incense. Let the smoke curl round and wisdom abound.

CAIT-SITH

The cait-sith is a fairy cat of Celtic folklore. As a spectral cat, it can be either good or bad luck, depending on where you see it. In Ireland, it was said to be a black cat with a white spot on its chest, and was considered bad luck. However, in the Highlands of Scotland it is more ambiguous. Here it is said to be a pure white spirit cat, with a spectral glow around it. While some believe it to be a bad omen, others claim it brings good fortune if it crosses your path. Another belief is that to see one by day is good luck, but by dark it bodes ill. Some say that the cait-sith will steal your soul as you sleep, while for others, she is a warning of someone holding harmful intent towards you. Whatever the truth, this simple spell will keep the cait-sith happy and your fortune good.

Cait-Sith Samhain Spell

On the night of Samhain (31st October in the northern hemisphere), take a saucer of fresh milk and place it on the doorstep. Next to this, place a few sprigs of dried catnip. Now repeat this blessing three times:

Cait-sith of fairy light

Bring no harm or ill this night

Accept these gifts of comfort and glee

Blessings be upon me and thee.

The magical Cait-Sith appears in different colours and is an omen of good or bad fortune.

GRIMALKIN

Another spirit cat, and cousin to the cait-sith, is the grimalkin. This Celtic legend could have been inspired by sightings of the Scottish wild cat. A grimalkin is a grey or grey-striped cat. It is said to be a trickster; it will befriend young children, though it doesn't like men! During the witch hunts of Scotland, grey cats, or grimalkins, were often thought to be witches in disguise, so cats of this colour became very distrusted and mistreated as a result. Legend states that grimalkins prefer the company of women and would frequently move in with solitary widows, adding fuel to the fire of the witch craze. Although not considered unlucky as such, if you were a woman living with a grey cat in the Highlands at the time, your odds of survival weren't that great! The grimalkin was so aligned with witches that 'grimalkin' became a derogatory term for an old lady or an outspoken woman. You can call on the grimalkin if you are being maligned in any way. Light a grey candle or a simple tealight and say:

Grimalkin, grimalkin uncross my path

Let those who malign me feel your wrath!

Ashes to ashes and dust to dust

The past dead and buried, free from mistrust

As I walk my own path, I will have my own say

Grimalkin protect me through each fight and fray.

CU-SITH

It isn't only cats that the Celts were superstitious about, but dogs too. The Cu-Sith is a fairy dog that tramps the Highlands and Islands of Scotland and Ireland. Some believe that he is a hound of the Wild Hunt, looking for prey, while others say he is simply out looking for unwary night-time travellers so he can steal their souls. He is a large hound, with a shaggy coat that has an unearthly greenish hue and green light coming from it, denoting his role as a fairy dog. His English counterparts would be the Barguest Hound, Black Shuck, the Grim and Old Padfoot. Like them, he is considered an omen of death or misfortune, so should you hear the sound of panting and heavy paws coming up behind you, it is said that you should take refuge in the nearest kirk, without looking back. Despite his bad reputation, he is nonetheless a messenger. He barks three times in warning; one bark indicates that the bad luck can be avoided, two barks that the misfortune is destined but a necessary lesson, while three barks is an omen of death. Like most hell-hound legends, the curse of the Cu-Sith can be thwarted by crossing a body of water, be it a loch, burn or stream, so all is not lost. Simply hop over a puddle and you're home and dry!

AULD NESSIE

Quite possibly the most famous Celtic beast of all is of course Auld Nessie, or the Loch Ness Monster. Nessie is an ancient water beast said

Some believe the Cu-Sith is a hound of the Wild Hunt.

Nessie is an ancient water beast said to reside in Loch Ness, Scotland.

to be living in the depths of Loch Ness in the Scottish Highlands. She was first sighted as far back as the 6th century by St. Columba. There have been many more sightings reported over the years, but some have proved to be no more than a hoax. That said, people still travel from across the globe for the chance of seeing Nessie breaching the surface of the loch, but she is a shy creature and tends to keep to the depths. However, legend states that offering her a wee dram in libation can improve your chances of making her acquaintance. Simply pour a small amount of whisky into the waters of Loch Ness and wait to see if you can spot the famous long neck and triple humps of Auld Nessie. Slainte!

Chapter Eight

CELTIC
ROMANCE

For all their warlike characteristics, the Celts also have a reputation for being quite romantic. In a landscape of majestic mountains and misty glens, of full moons rising over beautiful lochs or casting shadows on Pictish stones and ancient castles, it's hard *not* to become a romantic. The Celtic landscape simply oozes romance, and stories of star-crossed lovers, such as Scathach and Cucullain, are prolific in Celtic folklore.

This deep sense of romance infiltrates modern relationships too, with phrases such as 'taking the moonlight' and 'Anam Cara' (see below) being commonplace in Celtic regions. In this chapter we will explore some aspects of Celtic romance and look at ways in which you can invoke more of it in your own life. We begin with the Celtic view of soulmates…

ANAM CARA

Anam Cara is a Gaelic phrase that simply means 'soul friend', but there is far more to such a relationship than mere friendship. An Anam Cara relationship is complex, intense and frequently romantic in nature. Sexual tension is strong and ever present between the two parties. This is the Celtic version of twin flames, but with the added pressure that an Anam Cara relationship rarely runs smoothly.

There are often many obstacles in the way before the two lovers are free to be together, but once there, their commitment to one another is unshakable and everlasting.

This is because an Anam Cara relationship is thought to be a commitment the couple made in the spirit realms; a promise that their souls would find one another in this life, no matter what. This commitment means that all earthly obstacles become less significant, because it is *a love above all loves.*

While such obstacles might be inconvenient and frustrating, in the end the couple trust in the value of their love and in the fated success of an Anam Cara, spiritual bond. In short, they believe that they are destined to be together and nothing and no-one can prevent it.

Having said that, this type of relationship does have its drawbacks. Firstly, it cuts people off from other possibilities for romantic happiness as they are too invested in their Anam Cara – their *one true love.* Secondly it means that the couple have greater potential to hurt one another, because their investment is absolute, so the potential for heartbreak along the road to happiness is significant and something to consider. It is still a lovely concept though and something many people still aspire to.

If you want to draw your Anam Cara to you, cast the spell below, but be aware that such a love affair is not without its difficulties and the road ahead may be rocky before it leads you both to your happy ever after. Good luck!

Spell to Summon Your Anam Cara

Y ou will need two small paper hearts about 2cm square, one pink and one red, a red pen, a red candle, red thread and a sewing needle. As darkness falls, light the candle and say:

By burning flame my love is true

Wherever you are I call out to you

My Anam Cara, my Anam Cara, my Anam Cara.

Hold an image in your mind of your Anam Cara, your soul mate, and write your own name on the pink heart and the words Anam Cara on the red heart. Thread the needle and knot the end of the thread. Next pierce the pink heart from underneath, with your name facing upwards, using the needle and draw the thread through, right up to the knot. Say:

I pierce my own heart in love and light

To summon my Anam Cara to me on this night

Next pierce the red heart from underneath, with Anam Cara facing downwards and sandwiched with your name, and say:

I pierce my Anam Cara's heart in love and light

I summon him/her/them to me from this night.

Finally, remove the needle, wrap the remainder of the thread around the two hearts, and seal the end with a little melted wax from the candle. This is your love talisman, and it will help to draw your Anam Cara towards you and into your life. To complete the spell, hold tight to the hearts and repeat this chant nine times:

By burning flame these hearts are true,

Wherever you are I now summon you

My Anam Cara, my Anam Cara, my Anam Cara!

Keep the hearts with you at all times to draw your soul friend into your life. Allow the candle to burn down naturally.

The Fairy Lover

Of course, not everyone is looking for a love as intense as the Anam Cara variety. Some people are looking for something a bit more casual. A brief fling with a Fairy Lover might be just the ticket! In Celtic folklore the Fairy Lover is a fey companion who offers affection, adoration and sexual gratification for a limited time only. They seemingly appear out of nowhere and make an immediate beeline for their romantic target. The sabbats are a prime time to meet such a lover or to call one into your life for a brief encounter. They tend to disappear just as fast as they arrived and you will never hear from them again, for they have returned to the world of Elphame or the fairy realms. Their sudden appearance/disappearance is one of the signs that you have attracted the attentions of a Fairy Lover. They might also be extraordinarily good-looking and have green eyes or slightly pointed ears – clues as to their fey background.

A Fairy Lover isn't a lifelong companion. They are a brief encounter, an ego boost, a healing balm for a broken heart or an interlude to loneliness. They give you the confidence you need to get back in the game of love and romance. Like two ships that pass in the night, they will come when you have romantic need of them, never to be seen again. However, their magic will stay with you in the form of the sweet memories you made together and the confidence they imbued in you. Cast the following spell to summon a Fairy Lover into your life for a casual affair or a healing interlude.

Spell to Summon a Fairy Lover

This spell is most effective when cast into the sea by the light of the full moon, but any natural body of water will suffice. You will need a pebble. Hold this in your hand as you walk by the water, enjoying the sound of the lapping water or rolling waves. As you hold the pebble to your heart, close your eyes and imagine a fairy lover walking towards you and sweeping you off your feet. Now say the following incantation three times:

Galatea, Melusine, Aphrodite; Merrow Maids, all

Send out a Fairy Lover, to hold me in thrall

To thrill and delight me, to tantalize me

To heal and calm me, to offer sweet balm to me

To sweep me away before break of day

To love me and leave me but never deceive me

What once was yours I return to thee

As a Fairy Lover comes forth to me!

Throw the pebble into the water, preferably on the seventh wave of an incoming tide, and walk away from the water without looking back. Look out for your fairy lover, who should appear suddenly within seven days.

TAKING THE MOONLIGHT

'Taking the moonlight' is the act of courting outdoors. Being asked the question 'Will you take the moonlight with me tonight?' simply means will you meet up after dark for a kiss and a cuddle! While not everyone will be lucky enough to experience being courted among the misty glens, lochs and mountains of a Celtic landscape, you can nonetheless tap into this romantic tradition by casting this general love spell, inspired by the Celtic tradition of taking the moonlight.

Light a tealight and spend some time imagining your dream date. What would you wear, where would you go, how would you feel?

Picture it all, then when you are ready say the incantation below three times:

I summon a lover to explore the night

Together in love, taking the moonlight

I summon a lover to brighten my days

Together in joy, by sunshine haze

I summon a lover day by day

They move ever closer, coming my way.

I summon a lover to share the old ways

Taking the moonlight amid silver rays

So shall it be!

Let the tealight burn down and keep an eye open for romantic opportunities coming your way.

Auld Lang Syne Spell for a Lost Love

To get a second chance with a lost love write a note as to why you want to try with them again and what you have learnt from your mistakes. Burn this note and repeat the chant three times:

For Auld Lang Syne, for old time's sake

I spell of reunion I would make

Casting out through smoke and air

(Name) come back to me, good times to share

You will hear my call from miles away

Come back to me and return to stay

Spirit to spirit and heart to heart

No longer shall we be apart

I am dear to you, you are dear to me

Together again, so mote it be.

St. Andrew's Love Spell

S t. Andrew is of course the patron saint of Scotland and his saint's day is celebrated on the 30th of November each year. This traditional love spell calls on St. Andrew to bring about a love connection. It can be performed at any time on St. Andrew's Day. Light a tealight and write the following traditional incantation out on a slip of paper, then chant the words out loud three times in all:

I have a wish, a wish for a kiss

From a lover in a kilt, looking all fine

I cast this wish, this wish for a kiss

And by St. Andrew, this lover is mine!

Allow the tealight to burn down naturally and carry the spell paper with you wherever you go. Remember that love is always a surprise, so expect the unexpected and be open to new encounters – especially if they happen to be wearing a kilt!

Chapter Nine

BY ROOT AND BRANCH, LEAF AND TREE

The Celts had a strong affinity with trees, and the Druid priests would commune with them and use them in magic and divination. To the Celts, trees were more than just plants and vegetation; they were deities, with each tree signifying particular traits and omens. Trees provided fuel for the fire, wood for making weapons such as spears and bows, or currachs, which were the canoe-like boats used by the Celtic tribes. They offered shelter from harsh weather for livestock and sturdy thatch for croft-houses.

Vast parts of the Celtic regions were covered in great forests, from what is now the Black Forest in Germany to the great Caledonian and Snowdonian forests in the UK. Wildlife such as deer and boar could be hunted in the forest for meat, and the spirit of Cernunnos would have been honoured in the woods. The Druids would have foraged amid the trees for medicinal plants to heal their tribes, while the women and children would have picked berries and so on to formulate early dyes for cloth and wool. Trees were an intrinsic aspect of Celtic life and a vital resource for survival, so it is hardly surprising that the Celts invented their own 13-month calendar using trees, which we will explore shortly.

NEMETON GLADE: A SACRED GROVE

A nemeton is a scared place that offers a natural sense of sanctuary. Glades were open spaces within a glen or strath, while groves were clearings amid the forest, a space within the woods that was clear enough that you could light a fire without danger. Groves, glades and glens were nemetons, places to gather round for entertainment, war councils and debates. Here in the Grove, the Celts would have held celebrations and sabbat festivities. It was a place of power, where elders would pass on their wisdom, betrothals would be announced and youngsters would play, with the trees bearing witness.

We still feel echoes of the nemeton when we walk through a woodland and suddenly start to feel relaxed, uplifted, exhilarated and happy. Our troubles fall away and we enjoy being out in nature, in a sacred space surrounded by trees. That is the nemeton effect and it is one that our Celtic ancestors would have been very familiar with.

You can recreate this effect by planting trees around the edge of your garden if you have one, thus creating your own Grove and nemeton space for magic and meditation. Or use potted plants as an alternative. Consider planting trees that were sacred to the Celts, using their Tree Calendar as inspiration.

THE CELTIC TREE CALENDAR

For the Celts, the months of the year were ruled by trees. Here you can see that each tree was also attributed magical significance and energies.

BIRCH/BETH: 24 DEC. – 20 JAN.

The birch was considered a cleansing tree. Its bark would be burnt in a ritual fire to ward off bad luck, ill health or any blight on the livestock. It was also considered a transitional tree, marking the passing of the darkest time of year. In divination, the birch tree meant that you should reflect inwards and make a fresh start.

ROWAN/LUIS: 21 JAN. – 17 FEB.

Rowan is of course famous for being the *uncrossing* tree – that is, it is said to guard against witches and negative energies, although many witches actually use rowan in their spells to ward off bad vibes. An equal-armed cross of rowan twigs tied with red thread and hung outside the door to the house was said to prevent negative energies taking root in the home and protect the household from ill and bane.

ASH/FEARN: 18 FEB. – 17 MARCH

The Ash tree was thought to represent the three realms of past, present and future. It was therefore a fortune-telling tree and one that the Druids would meditate beneath to facilitate visions. A popular wood for Druid wands, the Ash Grove was said to be the most powerful nemeton of all.

ALDER/SAILLE: 18 MARCH – 14 APRIL

The Alder is the symbol of duality because it has both male and female catkins. It represents balance and polarity, light and dark, summer and winter. It reminds us that we cannot have one without the other, that life is governed by balance in all things. In divination, the alder tree would indicate that you need to redress the balance in your own life.

WILLOW/NION: 15 APRIL – 12 MAY

Willow is the tree of emotion, dreams and visions. It is flexible and so denotes that sometimes one must bend, so as not to be broken. It is about give and take, ebb and flow, the waxing and waning of the moon. A very feminine tree, the willow represents female strength and resilience. It is a message to trust your intuition and show compassion and empathy for others. It is the tree of kindness.

HAWTHORNE/HUATH: 13 MAY – 9 JUNE

This is a tree of protection, and wherever one grows, the area is protected by the goddess. Its thorns are sharp, its berries poisonous, and its blossom is the herald of spring. It is a very magical tree, and to cut one down is considered bad luck. However, to care for one and offer it regular libations of cider or ale is said to have the opposite effect, and will bring many blessings. It is, however, bad luck to bring hawthorn blossom into the house.

OAK/DUIR: 10 JUNE – 7 JULY

The tree of Cernunnos! The oak is symbolic of strength, wisdom and the Celtic god. To the ancient Druids, the regal oak was simply the King of the Woods and a tree that represented the sovereignty of the land. Oak trees were also considered portals, or doorways, to other realms. It is the tree most strongly associated with the months of summer.

HOLLY/TINNE: 8 JULY – 4 AUG.

The holly now marks the passing of summer and the return of the darker half of the year. Although strongly associated with winter, magically, the holly begins to come into its own in late summer. Again, it is a protective tree, and is said to bring good luck, especially if it bears many berries. Bringing holly into the home during the time of the winter solstice is said to protect the household throughout the depths of winter and the coldest months of the year. Offer the tree a libation in late summer and wassail it in winter to bring its blessings to you. As an evergreen tree of winter, it is linked to the Cailleach.

HAZEL/COLL: 5 AUG. – 1 SEPT.

The hazel tree was sacred to the Druids, who would eat the nuts to bring about prophetic visions. Hazelnuts were also fed to those who were about to be sacrificed. These trees are symbols of wisdom and the unknown. They represent prophecy, psychic visons and prophetic dreaming.

BRAMBLE/MUIN: 2 – 29 SEPT.

Bramble is the plant of resilience, stubbornness and obstinacy – and if you've ever tried to rid your garden of them, you will know why! Brambles are prickly and vicious, yet they also offer an abundance of autumn fruit, so they symbolise both sacrifice and prosperity. Bramble also symbolises fertility and virility. It is a plant that is strongest in the autumn months and is therefore associated with the autumnal equinox.

IVY/GORT: 30 SEPT. – 27 OCT.

Ever twining, ever binding, ivy symbolises dependence and smothering. It reminds us that there is a fine line between nurturing and suffocating! It is a warning not to become a clinging vine, but to maintain your independence. As an evergreen plant, it represents the Cailleach and her grip on the world in winter.

REED/NGETAL: 28 OCT. – 24 NOV.

Reeds were used as early writing implements, so this plant symbolises language, poetics, the written word and the scribe. They were also fashioned into pipes, so they symbolise musicality too. They represent knowledge, learning, academics, the Arts, studying and wisdom. Reed reminds us that we are always learning, every day, and that the quest for knowledge is never really over.

ELDER/RUIS: 25 NOV. – 23 DEC.

Elder, the magical thirteenth tree, is the tree of the Crone. It symbolises magic, spell-casting, healing, the fairy realms and the unknown. The Elder was a wise mother figure to the Celts and a symbol of the goddess. It was considered very bad luck to cut one down, though harvesting berries and blossoms was acceptable, providing one had asked the Elder Mother's permission first.

THE SACRED TRIAD

Whilst in England the sacred triad is made up of oak, ash and thorn, in Scottish Pecti Wita, the sacred triad is made up of thistle, heather and pine. Using these plants in your rituals is a good way to bring a touch of Wita to your spells, and each plant has its own special meaning.

The thistle is the emblem of Scotland. Its motto is 'None shall irritate me unscathed', and it is prickly enough to make its presence felt and administer immediate retribution if tampered with. In Wita, thistles were said to be masculine plants and were associated with the Horned God, Cernunnos. They are a visual reminder of strength, resilience and courage. Wearing thistle jewellery can help you to tap into these virtues.

Heather is a pretty flowering plant that grows in abundance across Scotland, turning the Highlands purple when in full flower. It is the feminine counterpart to the Scottish thistle, and is linked with the ancient queen Scotia, for whom Scotland is named. Wearing a sprig of heather is said to bring good fortune and ensure you are blessed by the Fae.

Scots pine is a fragrance we are all familiar with, as it is used to scent many products, from candles to bath salts. Pine grows abundantly in the rich Caledonian forests. There is great majesty to these trees, and the forests where they grow have a very special nemeton atmosphere. Burning pine incense or essential oil would help bring the spirit of Caledonia to your rituals.

The Clootie Tree

High on a hill in Inverness, overlooking the Cromarty Firth and Fort George, stands a colourful Clootie tree. This is a tree that has been made into a *wishing tree* by the local people. Tradition states that should you ever come across a clootie tree, you are entitled to request a single boon from the tree spirit. In return you must leave an item of clothing that you are wearing. To activate the boon, simply tie the item of clothing or clootie, meaning cloth, to a branch of the tree as you make your wish. Then walk away and do not look back. The spirit of the tree will grant your wish if it comes from the heart and causes no harm. The Clootie tree in Inverness is covered in scarves, gloves and socks, but you don't need to travel that far to tap into this old Celtic tradition. Simply find a friendly-looking tree and turn it into a Clootie tree by hanging the first item of clothing on its branches and making your wish. You could use a tree in your garden or a local woodland. This is an old tradition, similar to that of well dressing. The sabbats are always a good time to visit or create a Clootie tree; alternatively, visit the tree on the night of the full moon. Clootie trees are not exclusive to Scotland, so do some research and see if there is such a tree in your local area. If not, start a family tradition with a tree in your garden, or even with a sturdy houseplant on which you tie ribbons instead of clothing. In this way you are honouring the Celtic tradition of the magical wishing tree. Take special care of the tree and spend time tending it.

A Clootie tree with cloths tied to it representing wishes made.

Chapter Ten

WIND AND STONE

The Celts have left us a legacy of beautiful artwork and standing stones. These stones are generally carved with intricate designs known as Celtic knotwork, and totem animals such as eagles, stags, wolves and so on. Although the elements have weathered away some of these designs over the centuries, others can still be seen quite clearly.

The Eagle Stone in Strathpeffer in the Scottish Highlands is a Pictish stone that bears a carving of an eagle's head. Legend states that if this stone falls over three times, disaster will befall the town. This is typical of standing stones – there is always an accompanying legend or story to tell surrounding them. Other notable stones include the Ring of Brodgar, the Standing Stones of Callanish, the Nine Maidens Circle, Arbor Low Circle and Barrow Mound, and, of course, Stonehenge. People travel from all over the world to see these sacred sites. In this chapter we will look at the magic of stones and how they can be used in spell-craft to tap into the magic of the Celts.

THE CELTIC CROSS

One form of stone craft that is synonymous with the Celts is the cross. A Celtic Cross can be identified by the circle that is incorporated at the head of the cross and the intricate carvings that decorate it. It symbolises our connection with the earth and sky, the four winds and the four directions. For this reason, it is known as a cross that represents 'the parting and the meeting of the ways'. Celtic Crosses were often found at crossroads, and were popular meeting places. It is a symbol

An example of the traditional Celtic Cross.

older than Christianity, although it was adopted by early Christians and was displayed in kirks and churches. It is still a much beloved symbol, though it represents different things to different people. In Celtic magic it is a symbol of the four directions, their elements and associations, as follows:

North: The direction of Earth, symbolising abundance, prosperity and growth.

East: The direction of Air, symbolising intellect, new beginnings, creativity and communication.

South: The direction of Fire, symbolising passion, love, adventure and dynamic relationships.

West: The direction of Water, symbolising intuition, psychic powers, emotions and fluidity.

Celtic Cross Spell to Make a Decision

I f you have some kind of dilemma and you are not sure which way to turn, this simple spell can help you come to a decision. You will need a picture or drawing of a Celtic Cross, and a small feather. Hold the feather to your heart and say:

Pretty plume taking flight

Help me make the choice that's right.

Now concentrate on your dilemma and hold the feather over the cross. With your eyes closed, let the feather drop and see where it lands. Whatever part of the cross it lands on should determine your decision:

Body of Cross: stay rooted and do nothing for now. All will be revealed in time.

North: follow your own best interests, be practical and pragmatic.

East: follow your intellect, think things through carefully, weigh up pros and cons.

South: follow your heart, do what brings you joy, live passionately.

West: follow your dreams, go where they take you, trust in your talents.

Meeting of the Ways Spell for Reconciliation

Y ou can also use the symbolism of the Celtic Cross to bring about a reconciliation with someone you've lost touch with. Take an image of the cross and meditate on it for a few minutes – a Celtic Cross necklace would be perfect for this spell. Think of the person you wish to be back in contact with and say the following incantation as you gaze at the cross:

I saw you last at the parting of the ways

From there you left my side

I call you now, to the meeting of the ways

In lasting friendship to abide.

Keep the cross with you and, on a daily basis, touch it and say the name of your friend three times.

In My End Is My Beginning

Spirals are a popular Celtic design, because they have neither a defined end nor a beginning, but can be followed from either the centre or the outer limits and back again, like a labyrinth. Spiral spells are easy to cast and will look pretty on your altar, too. All you will need are thirteen stones or pebbles, a slip of paper and a pen.

You can use a spiral spell for both manifestation and banishing. Simply write your goal or objective on the piece of paper, fold it in half and place it beneath a stone, saying, 'such is my intention'. This stone is now your Intention Stone, so try to choose one that is easily identifiable from the rest.

To *manifest* your goal, place the rest of the stones in a spiral moving in a clockwise direction, making a clockwise spiral, with your intention stone at the centre. Alternatively, to *banish* something from your life, create a spiral in an anti-clockwise direction, using the intention stone as the final stone at the outer limits of the spiral, thus moving it away from you.

THE KEEK STONE

The keek stone is a scrying stone that was traditionally used by Pictish women and Druids as a tool of foresight. It is small and round, with a hole in the middle, hence it is sometimes known as a holey stone. To find a keek stone by the side of a loch is said to be lucky as it will protect the finder from all harm if they carry it with them. Such stones were threaded with string and worn around the neck as talismans. Women would sit by the side of the loch and look through the hole of the keek stone to scry in the waters beyond. The hole would act as a way to focus attention and filter the images and insights. The Brahan Seer was Scotland's answer to Merlin. He used a keek stone to tell the future, but so scandalous were his predictions that he was taken up on a charge of witchcraft and burned in a barrel at Chanonry Point in Inverness. Today there is a memorial stone there to commemorate him. These days we can use keek stones without fear. They are, however, notoriously hard to find but you can always make your own.

How to Make and Use a Keek Stone

To make your own holey stone you will need some modelling clay that fires in a conventional oven. Choose a colour that appeals to you, or one that looks pebble-like, such as grey or brown. You will also need a piece of string or ribbon, some incense, a rolling pin and a wooden clothes peg. First work the clay in your hands until it is malleable. Next roll it out into a small circle, about the size of a large pebble. Be sure not to roll it too thin – it needs to resemble a pebble. Now using the head of the wooden clothes peg, carefully push a hole through the middle of the clay to create a keek stone. Bake in the oven as directed. Once cooled, thread the keek stone onto the ribbon and pass it through incense smoke to bless it and cleanse it.

To use the stone for scrying, hold a question in your mind then peer through the stone, preferably looking out over water. Alternatively, you can peer through the keek stone into incense smoke. Use your intuition to decipher what images you see in the water or smoke. As with any kind of divination tool, scrying with a keek stone takes practice, so don't be downhearted if you find it difficult at first. Just keep on practicing.

Blessing of the Four Winds

This simple spell calls on the four winds to bring their blessings into your life. It is best performed out of doors.

Light a stick of your favourite incense and face east. Wave the incense and use your hand to pull the smoke towards you as you say:

Blessings of East and Air surround me,

Powers of communication and creativity all around me

Face south and repeat the process, saying:

Blessings of South and Fire surround me

Powers of love, passion and adventure all around me

Face west, pull the incense smoke towards you and say:

Blessings of West and Water surround me

Powers of intuition and ambition all around me

Finally, face north, repeat the process and say:

Blessings of North and Earth surround me

Powers of abundance and growth all around me.

Finish off the spell by dampening the ground with water and staking the incense stick in the earth as you say:

As I am blessed by the four winds,

So I leave this blessing in return

Blessed Be.

CONCLUSION

Mar sin leibh an-drasta!

Goodbye for now!

I hope that you have enjoyed this look at all things magical and Celtic! I have attempted to whet your appetite with history, mythology and magic. Although the Celts originated as a very Euro-centric culture, their influence is now felt globally and many people all over the world have a Celtic heritage and ancestry. This is something that connects us all, for we are all a part of one big clan – the Clan of the Celts. I trust that you have been inspired to learn more about your own links with the Celts and their influence on your country and culture, wherever you might live.

Remember that the past is always present, and you can tap into the power of Celtic mysticism whenever you want to. Bring the power of the Celts into your daily life by playing bagpipe music, wearing a kilt, observing Burns Night, and living your life like a modern Warrior Poet, regardless of gender. Be inspired by your ancestors, knowing that you are the current thread in a much larger tapestry of life. You can never be clan-less for your ancestors are watching over you. If you are tempted to visit any of the special places I have mentioned in this book, I trust that the magic you find there will stay with you for the rest of your days. May the road always rise to meet you and the path be smoothed before you.

Mar sin leibh an-drasta, or goodbye for now.
May Celtic blessings rain down upon you, until our next merry meeting!
Marie Bruce x

Spells Index

Further Reading

BOOKS

Scotland; A Concise History, Fitzroy Maclean

Scotland; Myths & Legends, Beryl Beare

The Jacobite Cause, Bruce Lenman

A History of Scotland, Neil Oliver

William Wallace; the Man and the Myth, Chris Brown

King and Outlaw; the Real Robert the Bruce, Chris Brown

An Anthology of Scottish Folk Tales, various authors

A Year of Scottish Poems, Gaby Morgan

A Gathering; a Personal Anthology of Scottish Poems, Alexander M Smith

Consider the Lilies, Iain Crichton Smith

Celtic Mythology, Arthur Cotterell

Celtic Wisdom, Andy Baggot

The Silver Bough, Marian McNeill

Celtic Wisdom, Caitlin Mathews

The Quest for the Green Man, John Mathews

The 21 Lessons of Merlyn, Douglas Monroe

Scottish Witchcraft, Raymond Buckland

By Oak, Ash and Thorn, D J Conway

Scottish Gaelic in Twelve Weeks, Roibeard O Maolalaigh & Iain MacAonghuis—this is a language book and CD tutorial set.

DVDS

A History of Scotland, Neil Oliver, BBC

The Celts, Blood, Iron and Sacrifice, Neil Oliver and Alice Roberts, BBC

Rise of the Clans, Neil Oliver, BBC

Blood of the Clans, Neil Oliver, BBC

Acknowledgements

With special thanks to my Bannockburn friend, Bob Beverage, for his knowledge of bagpipes and pipers in history, and for pointing me in the right direction.

This book is also for my soldiers at Fort George; Alan, Seamus and Hamish, and my Strathpeffer friend, Alexander.

With love to you all, always xxx

Picture Credits

Images courtesy of Shutterstock.

Image of Cernunnos on page 36 courtesy Bob Hilscher/Shutterstock.

Image of Gundestrup cauldron on page 38 courtesy Creative Commons.